RAILWAYS AROUND SELBY

Patrick Bennett

AMBERLEY

First published 2019

Amberley Publishing
The Hill, Stroud
Gloucestershire, GL5 4EP

www.amberley-books.com

Copyright © Patrick Bennett, 2019

The right of Patrick Bennett to be identified as
the Author of this work has been asserted in
accordance with the Copyrights, Designs and
Patents Act 1988.

ISBN 978 1 4456 8968 5 (print)
ISBN 978 1 4456 8969 2 (ebook)

British Library Cataloguing in Publication Data.
A catalogue record for this book is available from
the British Library.

Origination by Amberley Publishing.
Printed in the UK.

Contents

Introduction

Selby appeared early on the railway map of Britain. The Leeds & Selby was one of the very earliest railways to be built, and Selby station was the first to open in Yorkshire. The Hull & Selby followed not long after, giving a through route from Leeds to Hull. The line to Market Weighton followed shortly, and then in 1871, with the opening of the new East Coast Main Line, Selby became an important junction. It was at this time that the new loco shed was built. At the end of the century the Cawood, Wistow & Selby Railway came into being, followed a few years later by two late arrivals on the scene: the Selby to Goole line and the Derwent Valley Light Railway. The trains of the CWS eventually made their way into Selby station, while the DVLR shared a junction with the NER at Cliff Common, on the Market Weighton line.

Other important railways passed nearby. The Wakefield, Pontefract & Goole line remains today as an important freight artery serving the Aire Valley power stations. Not so lucky was the Hull & Barnsley Railway, which was closed almost in its entirety by the 1960s. In the same period the Beeching retrenchment saw the Selby to Goole and Selby to Market Weighton lines close. Before this, in 1959, the loco shed closed, victim of the increasing dieselisation of the railway. The CWS and DVLR both remained as goods lines long after their passenger services had ceased. The CWS finally succumbed in 1960, while the last remnant of the DVLR lingered on until 1981.

Selby lost a great deal of its importance with the diversion of the East Coast Main Line in 1983, following which the Selby–York line was closed. Despite all these closures Selby remains a busy station, probably seeing as many, if not more, passenger trains today as at any time in its history. Freight is a different story. As elsewhere, there has been a massive decline in goods traffic, particularly in traffic originating locally. Selby at one time had many local rail terminals. Today just two survive, both however generating regular flows. There is also a certain amount of through freight traffic.

Although having lost much of its former glory, Selby remains an interesting railway town with a complex and interesting history and it is that story that is recounted in these pages.

The author and publisher would like to thank the following people and organisations for permission to use copyright material in this book: the Transport Library for the photographs at Wistow, Selby, Selby BOCM, Barmby Moor, Carlton Towers, Drax and Monk Fryston; the Railway Correspondence and Travel Society for the photographs at Layerthorpe, Selby, Goole and Gascoigne Wood; the Industrial Railway Society for the photographs at Selby and Selby BOCM; Roger Griffiths for the photographs at Selby; Ben Brooksbank for the photographs at Selby, Barmby, Barlow, Goole and Bubwith; and Peter Groom for the photographs at Selby, Neville Hill and Goole.

Every attempt has been made to seek permission for copyright material used in this book. However if we have inadvertently used copyright material without permission/acknowledgement we apologise and we will make the necessary correction at the first opportunity.

Patrick Bennett
Selby, September 2019

The Leeds & Selby Railway

The idea of a railway between Leeds and Selby was discussed as early as 1814. The idea was revived in 1821 as a Leeds to Hull railway. In 1824 the Leeds & Hull Railroad Company was formed and George Stephenson was appointed as engineer. His proposal was for a double-track railway with three inclined planes worked by stationary engines to surmount the hills out of Leeds. The idea came to nothing, but in 1826 the Knottingley & Goole Canal was opened and the Hull shareholders were fearful of the loss of traffic to the port to Goole. The railway project was revived but it was decided that it would extend only from Leeds to Selby, where goods and passengers would be transferred to a packet boat for the rest of the journey to Hull. Today this may seem a strange idea but prior to the coming of the railways the most efficient form of travel was by canal or river. Travel by road was extremely slow and expensive. To travellers at the time, a waterborne journey would be nothing exceptional.

Having abandoned the idea of inclined planes, the only major constructional feature of the line was the 700-yard-long Richmond Hill tunnel just outside Leeds. The majority of this tunnel was later opened out, leaving today just 118 yards still in tunnel. Shortly after leaving Leeds the line rose for 4 miles at a maximum gradient of 1 in 153 to a point between Crossgates and Garforth. It was then level for 2 miles before falling for 6 miles at a maximum gradient of 1 in 136, after which it was level as far as Selby. There were stations at Leeds Marsh Lane, Crossgates, Garforth, Roman Road, Micklefield, Milford, Hambleton and Selby. Old maps show a goods station at Thorpe Gates but there was probably never anything more than a siding. There were forty-three bridges and sixteen level crossings. The Roman Road station lasted only two months; having opened with the railway on 22 September 1834, it closed on 10 November.

By 22 September 1834 a single line had been completed and the railway was officially opened. The opening was a grand event with 20,000 people turning

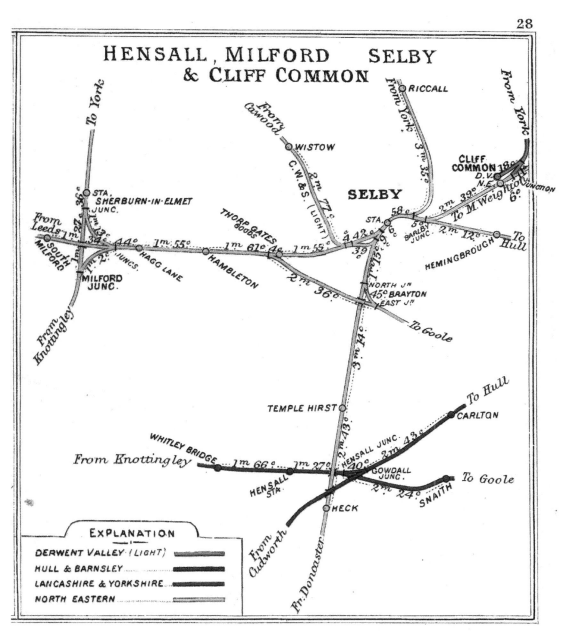

A Railway Clearing House map of the Selby area.

out to witness the first train, which was hauled by 2-2-0 *Nelson*, built by Fenton, Murray & Jackson. Unfortunately the engine struggled on wet rails on the climb out of Leeds and the journey to Selby eventually took some two and a half hours. The return journey was accomplished in seventy-six minutes. Apart from *Nelson*, other locomotives, also 2-2-0s, were supplied by Edward Bury.

These were not up to the job and were soon sold, being replaced by further machines from Fenton, Murray & Jackson, and later by Thomas Kirtley, all being either 2-2-0s or 2-2-2s. By December 1834 the second line had been laid and the railway was able to commence normal operation, which consisted of two return services per day.

The terminus at Selby was designed by James Walker, the railway's engineer, and built by Atack & Boothman, who also built the Leeds terminus. The building consists of a three-span train shed, the roof supported by timber trusses borne on cast-iron columns. The two inner lines were for passengers, while the two outer pairs were for freight. These lines passed out of the back of the building onto jetties alongside the River Ouse where goods were transhipped to riverboats. As for passengers, they had to make their own way to a landing stage in order to continue their journey to Hull by water. The two outer walls of the building were some 2 feet thick. The plan was to build warehouses adjoining the station for which they would have constituted one of the walls. In the event the warehouses were never built.

The building only remained in use as a station until 1840, after which it became a goods shed. In 1841 two more openings were made in the end wall and the former passenger lines were extended on to the jetty. Additional buildings were added on both sides but the original building remains substantially intact. Today it is no longer in railway use but remains as a warehouse. It is one of the most important early railway buildings in Britain and is a listed structure.

In May 1839 George Hudson's York & North Midland Railway opened from York to a point near Milford station, where a short chord connected it to the L&S. In November 1840, Hudson, fearing competition from rival companies using the L&S line, arranged to lease the L&S for £17,000 per annum. Hudson immediately closed the L&S west of Milford, compelling trains to use his route into Leeds, despite it being 4 miles longer. Passenger services along this section were reinstated in 1850. In 1844 the L&S was absorbed into the Y&NM, which ten years later became the North Eastern Railway.

Of the original stations, Cross Gates, Garforth, Micklefield and Milford (renamed South Milford) remain open. In 1930 Osmondthorpe station opened, closing again in 1960. Hambleton closed in 1959 and East Garforth was opened in 1987 to serve new housing estates. In 1922, the last year of the NER's existence, there were eight trains daily between Leeds and Selby, one of these to/from Liverpool. In 1947, the last year of the LNER's existence, there were fourteen trains daily between the two cities, with additional services on Saturdays.

The first station at Selby. The two outer doors are original. These allowed the egress of freight wagons onto the quay. The two central doors (one now bricked up) were added in 1841 when the station became wholly used for freight. The building on the left is a later addition.

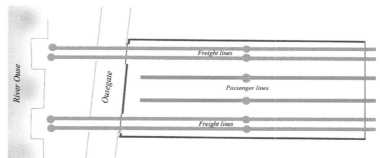

The layout of the first Selby station.

The remains of the landing stage whereby passengers gained access to the packet boats for onward travel to/from Hull.

B1 4-6-0 No. 61237 *Geoffrey H Kitson* passes Selby loco shed as it heads off in the Leeds direction on 23 May 1959. (Photo N. Stead, courtesy of The Transport Library)

EWS locomotive No. 66134 approaches Thorpe Gates level crossing on 5 May 2001 with a train of Polybulk wagons.

A TransPennine Class 185 'Desiro' unit rounds the curve from the Leeds line as it arrives at Selby with a Manchester Piccadilly–Hull service on 16 July 2018.

The Hull & Selby Railway

It was soon apparent that transport between Leeds and Hull, with transhipment at Selby, was less than satisfactory. The onward journey to Hull could take up to five hours. Hull businessmen were concerned by the rise of Goole as a port and the threat of new railways to Bridlington and Scarborough. The Hull & Selby Railway Company was formed in 1834 and an Act obtained in 1836. The terrain over which the line was to be built was almost completely flat with very few obstacles. The maximum gradient was 1 in 240 and 9.63 miles of the 30.75 miles were completely flat. The main engineering challenges were the crossing of the Ouse at Selby, and bridges across the River Derwent and the Market Weighton Canal.

From Selby, where junction was made with the Leeds & Selby, the line crossed the Ouse by means of a bascule bridge and curved away to the east

The seal of the Hull & Selby Railway.

before running in a straight line to Brough. From here it followed the Humber, eventually turning north into the centre of Hull. There were intermediate stations at Cliff, Howden, Eastrington, Staddlethorpe, Brough, Ferriby and Hessle. Wressle was opened later. Cliff was renamed Hemingbrough in 1874. A new station was built at Selby and the old station became the goods shed. The 1836 authorising Act required the bascule bridge to have an opening of 44 feet. The cast-iron bridge consisted essentially of two main spans, one of which opened, together with the approaches on either side, being a total of 190 feet long. Opening of the bridge was worked manually by turning a 9-foot diameter wheel. The bridge was completed by March 1840.

The track was unusual. It consisted both of sections of line laid conventionally on transverse sleepers, with other sections on sleepers laid longitudinally under the rails. These latter sections were to give trouble and were later replaced by conventional track. It may be remembered that Brunel on the Great Western used longitudinal timbers under the rails on his broad gauge, and also experienced problems.

Six locomotives were provided by Fenton, Murray & Jackson, and three by Shepherd & Todd, who later provided a further machine. When the line opened on 1 July 1840 it was four of the Fenton machines that hauled the initial trains from Hull. These were *Selby*, *Exley*, *Andrew Marvel* and *Kingston*. Return journeys from Selby started at 4 p.m., after which there was a celebratory dinner, attended by amongst others George Hudson.

The line was immediately profitable, returning a dividend of 2.5 per cent. In 1845 the H&S was proposing to build a line from Hull to Bridlington. Hudson, the chairman of the York & North Midland, was also proposing to build a line to Bridlington, in his case from Scarborough. In order to avoid competition Hudson proposed to lease the H&S. It will be remembered that he had already done likewise with the Leeds & Selby. The lease was agreed and came into effect on 1 July 1845. The following year a new lease was agreed, this time intended to make the Y&NM and the Leeds & Manchester joint lessors. However, it later transpired that the L&M (later to become the Lancashire & Yorkshire) had never taken up the lease. The NER, as successor to the Y&NM, continued to lease the H&S until 1872, at which time it became fully absorbed into the NER.

The increasing number of trains and their increasing weight led to the installation of a new bridge across the Ouse in 1891. The new bridge, which was built slightly to the east of the bascule bridge, was contracted to Nelson & Co. of York. The hydraulic machinery was from Armstrong Mitchell, and the ironwork by the Cleveland Bridge & Engineering Co. The bridge has an asymmetric swinging span of 130 feet and a fixed span of 110 feet. The swinging span is centred on the north bank, where there is also the accumulator

The bascule bridge across the Ouse at Selby.

HULL AND SELBY, OR HULL AND LEEDS JUNCTION, RAILWAY.

OPENING OF THE LINE

FOR PASSENGERS AND PARCELS ONLY,

ON THURSDAY, JULY THE 2nd, 1840

THE Public are respectfully informed that this RAILWAY will be OPENED THROUGH-OUT from HULL to the JUNCTION with the LEEDS and SELBY RAILWAY, at Selby, on WEDNESDAY, the First Day of July next, and that PASSENGERS and PARCELS only will be conveyed on THURSDAY, July 2nd ; thus presenting a direct Railway Conveyance from Hull to Selby, Leeds, and York without change of Carriage.

TRAINS WITH PASSENGERS WILL START FROM HULL AS UNDER

AT SEVEN O'CLOCK, A.M | AT THREE O'CLOCK, P.M.
AT TEN O'CLOCK, A.M. | AT SIX O'CLOCK, P.M.
ON SUNDAYS, AT SEVEN O'CLOCK, A.M., AND SIX O'CLOCK, P.M.

The Trains from LEEDS and YORK, for HULL, will depart from those Places at the same Hours ; and Passengers and Parcels may be Booked through at the Leeds, York, and Hull Stations. Arrangements are also in progress for Booking Passengers to Sheffield, Derby, Birmingham, and London.

THE FARES TO BE CHARGED ARE AS UNDER :

	First Class.	Second Class.	Third Class.
Hull to Selby	4s. 6d.	4s. 0d.	2s. 6d.
Hull to York	8s. 0d.	6s. 6d.	4s. 6d.
Hull to Leeds	8s. 0d.	6s. 6d.	4s. 6d.

No Fees are allowed to be taken by the Guards, Porters, or any other Servants of the Company.

The Trains, both up and down, will call at the Stations on the Line, viz. :—Hessle, Ferriby, Brough, Staddlethorpe, Eastrington, Howden, and Cliff.

Arrangements for carrying Goods, Cattle, Sheep, &c., will be completed in a short time, of which due Notice will be given.

By Order,

GEORGE LOCKING, Secretary.

Railway Office, Hull, June 24th, 1840.

Poster advertising the opening of the H&S line.

tower for the hydraulic engines. The hydraulic pressure was originally supplied by a steam engine, later replaced by electric power. The control cabin was situated atop the swinging span. The tracks of the converging lines from Hull and York were gauntleted across the bridge. In 2013 the bridge was completely refurbished, now being electrically controlled, with the equipment located in the accumulator tower.

The opening of the new East Coast route in 1871 led to the rebuilding of Selby station. This was completed by Thomas Nelson in 1873 to the design of Thomas Prosser, the NER company architect. The station was further modified in 1891 in conjunction with the opening of the new bridge. The west platforms were retained, while the east platforms were moved eastwards, reusing and extending Prosser's platform roof.

Hemingbrough station closed in 1967. Wressle and Eastrington were also proposed for closure under the Beeching plan but have managed to survive. Although they have survived they have a very sparse service. Wressle gets a couple of trains in the morning and evening peaks and Eastrington just one return service per day. The other intermediate stations between Selby and Hull have a varied service pattern. The seven daily Hull Trains Kings Cross–Hull services all call at Howden and Brough. The TransPennine Express services call at Brough and some at Howden also. At the eastern end of the line the

The swing bridge of 1891, which replaced the bascule bridge.

The control cabin atop the swing bridge.

Gilberdyke to Hull stations have an hourly service provided by trains to/from Sheffield or Doncaster. The Northern Trains York–Hull services all call at Howden, Gilberdyke and Brough. The intermediate stations between Selby and Leeds are served by the York–Hull and the Leeds–Selby trains, giving them a twice-hourly frequency. The hourly TPE Manchester Piccadilly–Hull trains also call at Garforth.

Today's service compares very well with the service provided at the end of the nineteenth century, often cited as a golden age for rail transport. At that time there were fifteen services daily between Leeds and Selby, ten of them semi-fast, plus three trains from Selby to Hull. Today on weekdays, passengers on both the Leeds & Selby Railway and the Hull & Selby Railway enjoy no fewer than thirty-nine services daily between those towns.

Hemingbrough station seen in 1989, when the signal box was still active. The station closed in 1967.

The station building at Howden. It is no longer in railway use, although the station remains open.

D49/2 4-4-0 No. 62761 *The Derwent* arrives at Selby on 5 April 1957 with a local from Hull. Notice the lower quadrant signals on the left. No. 62761 was withdrawn from service later that year. (Photo Ben Brooksbank)

On 31 March 1990 unit No. 156467 passes Gilberdyke Junction signal box with the 12.15 Manchester Piccadilly to Hull. The lines on the left lead to Goole. Gilberdyke Junction signal box has now been abolished.

In July 2018 a Class 158 unit passes through Barlby loops with a York–Hull service.

The Wakefield, Pontefract & Goole Railway

In the 1840s there were four proposals before Parliament for a line connecting Goole to the railway system. They were the Brayton & Goole, proposed by Hudson (this line was eventually built but not until 1912); the Goole & Doncaster; the Barnsley & Goole; and the Wakefield, Pontefract & Goole. The latter was supported by the Manchester & Leeds, which put up half the capital, and the railway received its Act in July 1846. As well as the 26-mile-long main line, there were to be three branches. These were Pontefract to Methley, Knottingley to Askern and Oakenshaw to the North Midland Railway. Stations were to be provided at Wakefield Kirkgate, Sharlston, Crofton, Featherstone, Tanshelf, Pontefract, Knottingley, Whitley Bridge, Hensall, Snaith, Rawcliffe and Goole.

The first sod was turned by Mr Pemberton-Milnes on 1 August 1846 and the main line opened on 29 March 1848, by which time the WP&G was part of the L&M, which had by then changed its name to the Lancashire & Yorkshire Railway, which could now boast a line from coast to coast – Liverpool to Goole. On that date a train of twenty-four coaches hauled by two locomotives left Wakefield. At Pontefract a further twenty-six coaches, together with another engine, were added and the train proceeded to Goole amid much celebration. The passing of the years saw a gradual increase in the frequency of services on the eastern half of the line, from five return services in 1858, to seven in 1872 – the majority now using the NER station in Goole, which had opened in 1869 – to nine or ten in 1887 and twelve in 1895. Of these, the majority continued through to Hull and three were semi-fasts. Journey time for the stopping trains was seventy-five minutes. There were two trains on Sundays. The interwar years saw a similar number, which was reduced to six or seven during the second conflict. In 1957 there were eight return trains per day, taking seventy-one minutes, thus a reduction in journey time of just four minutes after more than fifty years of progress!

All the stations on the line were proposed for closure under the Beeching plan, although the line itself was not. This was undoubtedly due to the heavy freight traffic, consisting of twenty-five to thirty freight trains each way daily. Somehow the stations remained open and there was still a good service in 1966, with ten trains each way. It was a different story by 1991, when there were just three trains one way and two the other. The current service (2018) consists of just a morning and an evening train from Goole to Leeds, and an evening train from Leeds to Goole. Freight traffic today consists almost entirely of trains to and from Drax Power Station, with up to fifty workings in a twenty-four-hour period. Apart from this there are one or two empty stock workings.

East of Knottingley, which is the section of line with which this book is concerned, the railway is a shadow of its former self. Just before Knottingley is the freight-only Askern branch, which connects to the ECML and Shaftholme Junction. There were once stations on this line at Womersley, Norton and Askern, all of which closed in 1948. In the angle between the Goole line and the Askern line is Knottingley Traction Maintenance Depot, opened in 1967 to provide motive power principally for the 'merry-go-round' (MGR) trains to the Aire Valley power stations. At England Lane there was once a coal depot. Continuing east, we come to Sudforth Lane and the sidings for the now closed Kellingley Colliery. Next is Whitley Bridge station, followed shortly by the junction for Eggborough power station, currently out of use.

Hensall station is a remarkable survivor, little changed from the time of its construction. Around three-quarters of a mile further on, the railway passes under the ECML. When the direct route between Doncaster and York was first opened in 1871, a north to east chord was put in. However, it received little use and later closed. Next comes Drax Branch Junction, formerly Hensall Junction, the branch for the mighty Drax Power Station, one of the last remaining fragments of the Hull & Barnsley Railway. Just beyond here the H&B main line crossed, followed by the GC&H&B Jt line. This line opened in 1916 and was equipped with platforms for a number of stations. However, the stations never opened. Beyond Drax Branch Junction the line becomes single track. Snaith station has been reduced to a single platform with a small shelter. There is an interesting display in the car park showing scenes from the railway's past. Next comes Rawcliffe station and finally the line joins the Doncaster–Goole line at Potters Grange Junction, shortly before Goole station.

Knottingley Motive Power Depot in 1992. Class 08 and 56 locos predominate.

The 'Swiss Cottage'-style Hensall station, a building dating from the opening of the line. It has survived remarkably unchanged. This photograph was taken in 1990.

Rawcliffe station, in a view taken probably in the early part of the twentieth century.

Rawcliffe station, seen in 2018. It would be difficult to imagine a station with more minimal facilities: just a short length of platform and not even a waiting shelter. Happily, the rather nice station house survives.

On 18 July 2002 Pacer No. 142065 passes England Lane with one of the very few services each day to Goole. In the background is Ferrybridge Power Station.

At the same location but travelling in the opposite direction is EWS loco No. 66042 with a rake of empty coal wagons from Drax Power Station.

Further to the east, at Sudforth Lane, Freightliner loco No. 66560 passes with yet another coal train.

The Selby & Driffield Railway

In June 1845 the Hull & Selby was authorised to build a line from Hull to Bridlington. The company was also surveying lines from Bridlington to York via Market Weighton, and Market Weighton to Selby. It will be remembered that about this time the York & North Midland had taken out a lease on the H&S and in fact it was the Y&NM that built these lines. The Selby line was authorised by an Act of 18 June 1846. No great difficulties were experienced building the line, which was across almost entirely flat terrain, and it was intended that it should open in November 1847. However, delays were caused by disagreements over the siting of stations, not least involving Revd Jefferson of Bubwith, who wanted the local station sited to the east of the village. To appease him, some time later another station, High Field, was built less than a mile away to the east. The railway eventually opened on 1 August 1848. The single track was mostly level, except when nearing Market Weighton, where gradients of 1 in 101/204 were encountered. There were eighteen level crossings in the 16.5 miles between Barlby Junction and Market Weighton. There were stations at Cliff Common Gate, Duffield Gate, Menthorpe Gate, Bubwith, Foggathorpe Gate, Holme and Harswell Gate. High Field station, mentioned above, was included in timetables from 1859. 'Gate' was later removed from the names of Cliff Common and Foggathorpe. Harswell Gate was renamed Everingham in 1874. Duffield Gate was closed in 1889 and Holme renamed Holme Moor in 1923.

It had always been intended that the line would be extended beyond Market Weighton to Driffield. However, the Y&NM showed no inclination to build this extension; nor did the NER when it absorbed the Y&NM in 1854. The years went by and finally in 1884 an independent company, the Scarborough, Bridlington & West Riding Junction Railway, proposed a line from Scarborough, bypassing Bridlington, to Driffield, and from there to Market Weighton and on to Howden on the Selby–Hull line. In the end only

Market Weighton station, seen in 1940. The NER built a number of stations in this overall roof design. (Photo courtesy East Riding Archives)

the Driffield–Market Weighton section was built and the line was worked from the outset by the NER. The line was opened on 21 April 1890. There were intermediate stations at Enthorpe, Middleton-on-the-Wolds, Bainton and Southburn. This line was a different proposition to the mostly flat line between Selby and Market Weighton. After the latter station the line climbed at 1 in 97/100 to a summit at Enthorpe, after which it fell at similar gradients towards Driffield. It was at this time that the Selby–Market Weighton line was doubled. The SB&WRJR was absorbed by the NER in 1914.

The initial service between Selby and Market Weighton was two trains per day. By 1866 there were four, one of which did not stop at Duffield Gate, Menthorpe Gate or Harswell Gate. Only the last train of the day was exclusively for passengers, the others being mixed. The passenger-only train took fifty minutes; the others up to an hour and a quarter. The timetable of 1895 shows a total of ten trains between Selby and Market Weighton, most of which started back at Leeds. Seven of these continued through to Bridlington, the other three terminating at Market Weighton. Three of the trains were fast between Selby and Market Weighton, taking just twenty-three minutes. The stopping trains took around forty-five minutes.

On the eve of the First World War the service pattern and running times were broadly similar, although during the war itself services were halved. Services continued much as before during the interwar period. During this period

A very early photograph of Cliff Common station. The locomotive is one of Alexander McDonnell's '38' Class of 4-4-0s, introduced in 1884.

Everingham station, a very typical G. T. Andrews standard design.

In the same style is Foggathorpe. One very characteristic feature of Andrews's designs was the 'Siamesed' chimneys.

Sentinel steam railcars were used for a time between Selby and Bridlington. During the Second World War there were just three passenger trains daily, with considerably extended journey times. The summer timetable of 1947 shows just a morning and evening return service between Selby and Bridlington, together with a Mondays-only Holme Moor to Selby service, for Selby market day. On Saturdays there were several through trains from Leeds, York and Manchester to Bridlington and Filey (for the holiday camp). By October 1950 there were three trains from Selby to Bridlington stopping at all stations, plus the Selby market day train from Holme Moor. Frequent performers on these services were the venerable 4-4-0s of Classes D17 and D20, both dating to the turn of the century. Later, Class D49s from Selby and Bridlington were used.

During the 1950s there was considerable holiday and excursion traffic passing along the line, often hauled by B16 4-6-0s. As an example, on summer Saturdays in 1957 there were thirty-eight additional services using the line to get through to Bridlington. However, traffic from the intermediate stations was minimal so it came as no surprise when first Menthorpe Gate closed in 1953, with the others following in 1954. Enthorpe closed to goods in 1959, and apart from Holme Moor and Everingham, which closed in 1965, the rest closed to goods in 1964. A minimal passenger service remained until final closure in June 1965.

Quite commonly used on the Selby–Market Weighton trains were the D20 4-4-0s designed by Wilson Worsdell. No. 62343 is seen at Selby loco shed on 11 July 1956. (Photo Peter Groom)

Also used were Worsdell's earlier D17 4-4-0s. In NER days No. 1871 stands alongside Selby coal stage. (Photo courtesy of The Transport Library)

Bubwith station, looking towards Market Weighton. A view dating from 1961. (Photo Ben Brooksbank)

Just to the east of Bubwith station the railway crossed the River Derwent by this viaduct.

These are the platforms of Foggathorpe station. Happily, a long section of the Selby–Market Weighton line survives as a footpath, 'The Bubwith Rail Trail'.

To the east of Market Weighton the railway divided, one line going to Driffield and the other to Beverley. This latter has also become a footpath with some interesting railway remains. This is Kiplingcotes signal box.

Cherry Burton station, now a private house.

Routes North –
The East Coast Main Line

The origin of the North Midland Railway lay in the desire of the merchants of Leeds to have an outlet for their goods to the south, and particularly to London. Once the NMR was built between Leeds and Derby, this would be achieved by using the Midland Counties Railway between Derby and Rugby, and the London & Birmingham between Rugby and London. The NMR was built to the plans of George Stephenson and rather unfortunately passed through no place of consequence on its 40-mile length. The MCR opened on 30 May 1839 and the NMR on 1 July 1840. Concurrent with the construction of the NMR was the building of the York & North Midland Railway, which connected with the NMR at Normanton. It also opened on I July and thus for the first time there was a through route from York to London. The MCR and the NMR, together with the Derby & Birmingham, would later merge to form the Midland Railway.

The next railway on the scene was the Great Northern, which, despite considerable opposition from the Midland, received its Act on 26 June 1846. Its line ran from London to Askern Junction, just beyond Doncaster. Between Askern Junction and York it had running powers first on the Lancashire & Yorkshire line to Knottingley, and thence via the North Eastern Railway to Burton Salmon and on to York.

In 1864 the NER received an Act authorising it to build two new lines. The first was from Chaloners Whin Junction to Barlby, just to the east of Selby on the Hull & Selby line, and the second was from just south of Selby to Shaftholme Junction. The two new lines opened on 2 January 1871. For the next 112 years this formed part of the East Coast Main Line.

It can be imagined how pleased the British Railways Board was when the National Coal Board proposed the building, at its own expense, of a brand-new

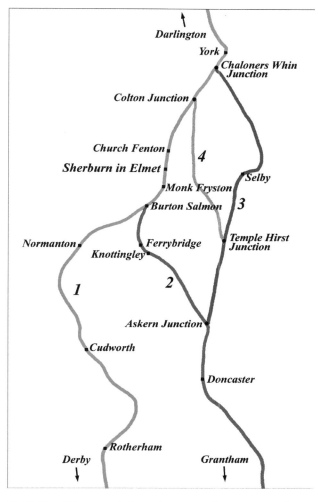

Routes to the north.

125 mph line as part of the ECML. The need for this new line arose from the desire of the NCB to exploit the Selby Coalfield, which extended under the ECML north of Selby. Such exploitation would have been likely to cause subsidence and thus a diversionary line avoiding the area was proposed by the NCB. The proposal was first put forward by the NCB in 1974 but it was 1980 before work started, being completed in 1983. The 13.79-mile-long line runs from Colton Junction to Temple Hirst Junction. It was built for 125 mph running and cost a total of £63 million. At that time there were no stations open between Selby and York and it was decided to close the ECML between Barlby and Chaloners Whin Junction. The only inconvenience was caused to the local traffic between Selby and York but these trains could now travel along the Leeds & Selby line as far as Hambleton, where a chord took them on to the new route and thence to York. The major gain for the railway was the avoidance of the speed restriction and swing bridge at Selby.

Ferrybridge and Knottingley station on the 1850 route to the north.

North of Ferrybridge is Sherburn in Elmet.

Church Fenton Ry. Station.

Church Fenton is at the junction of the lines to Leeds and to Burton Salmon. Its importance is reflected in the grandeur of the station. Sadly, this has now all been swept away, leaving just bare platforms.

Monk Fryston was a station between Sherburn in Elmet and Ferrybridge. In 1958 B1 4-6-0 No. 61295 hurries through with a southbound passenger train. The station closed the following year. (Photo N. Stead, courtesy of The Transport Library)

On the 1871 route between Selby and York there were stations at Naburn, Escrick and Riccall. This is Escrick, which closed in 1953.

At Riccall, a C1 4-4-2 'Large Atlantic' passes southbound with a mixed freight. Riccall station closed in 1958.

Another closed station on the East Coast route is Temple Hirst. Temple Hirst Junction is where the 1983 diversionary route rejoins the 1871 ECML.

Until 1983 the main East Coast route passed through Selby. On 20 June 1959 A4 Pacific No. 60020 *Guillemot* passes through the station with an up express. (Photo N. Stead, courtesy of The Transport Library)

Powering away from York on 31 August 1981 with the 09.50 Edinburgh to Plymouth is 'Peak' No. 45137 *The Bedfordshire and Hertfordshire Regiment (TA)*.

'Deltic' No. 55021 *Argyll and Sutherland Highlander* is seen at Bishopthorpe, between York and Selby, with the 14.03 Kings Cross to York on 31 August 1981.

On 10 September 1981 'Deltic' No. 55017 *The Durham Light Infantry* leaves Selby with a Dundee–Kings Cross service.

On the same day, further south at Brayton Junction, 'Deltic' No. 55008 *The Green Howards* passes with the 10.47 York to Kings Cross.

On 10 July 2018 a Hull Trains 'Adelante' unit departs from Selby with a service for Kings Cross.

The Hull & Barnsley Railway

There is a rule of thumb about railway closures, which is that the last to be built were often the first to close. Later lines often served smaller communities or were to some extent duplicate lines. Both cases are true of the Hull & Barnsley Railway. The impetus for the building of the H&B lay in the resentment of the predominant position of the NER regarding the traffic to the port of Hull. At a meeting at the Station Hotel in Hull a plan was put forward for both a railway and a new dock. Thus it was that the Hull, Barnsley & West Riding Junction Railway & Dock Company was formed. Its main activity was to be the transport of coal from the South Yorkshire coalfields to a new dock at Hull. The Act received royal assent on 26 August 1880. Construction took five years and was even halted at one point due to lack of funds. The line had cost more than double the original estimate to build.

After leaving Hull the line climbed at gradients up to 1 in 100 to reach the 2,116-yard-long Drewton Tunnel. The line then fell for 7 miles at 1 in 150, passing through Sugar Loaf and Weedley tunnels to reach North Cave. From here the terrain was flat as far as Kirk Smeaton, after which the land became hilly again. There were two more tunnels, at South Kirby and at Brierley, before the end of the line was reached at Cudworth. There were more than a hundred bridges, including the swing bridges across the River Hull and the Ouse near Drax. The line was 53 miles long and there were stations at Hull Cannon Street, Beverley Road, Willerby and Kirkella, Little Weighton, South Cave, North Cave, Wallingfen, Sandholme, Eastrington, Howden, Barmby, Drax, Carlton, Kirk Smeaton, Upton and North Elmsall, Hemsworth and South Kirby, and Cudworth. Despite its main business being the transport of coal and other goods, the H&B stations were substantial and attractive brick-built structures. One notable feature was the unusually wide platforms, with their equally wide decorative canopies. The H&B crossed numerous lines of other companies. At Eastrington it met the NER Selby–Hull line, giving the inhabitants of the village the choice of two stations just half a mile apart. At Drax the NER Selby–Goole line was met and at Hensall there was a junction with the L&Y Knottingley–Goole line. Shortly after this, the ECML was crossed and then the L&Y Askern branch.

Alexandra Dock opened on 16 July 1885, freight traffic started four days later and passengers were first carried on the 27th. The timetable of 1895 shows six trains through to Cudworth, three as far as Carlton, two of these continuing to Knottingley, and one service only as far as North Cave. On Sundays there was one train to/from Cudworth and one to Knottingley. The previous year the South Yorkshire Junction Railway came into being. This was a branch from Wrangbrook Junction to Denaby and Conisbrough. The line was worked from the outset by the H&B. There were stations at Pickburn and Brodsworth, and Sprotborough, and a service of two trains per day between Carlton and Denaby and Conisbrough was instituted from the 1 December 1894. This service lasted only until February 1903. In 1902 the Hull & South Yorkshire Extension Railway was opened, which ran from Wrangbrook Junction to Wath. There were stations at Moorhouse and South Elmsall, and Hickleton and Thurnscoe. Passenger trains ran between Kirk Smeaton and Wath. In 1905 the company simplified its name to the Hull & Barnsley Railway.

The Hull & Barnsley was noted for the grandeur of its stations, despite serving small communities, as here at Howden. Howden became South Howden following the merger of the H&B and NER.

HULL & BARNSLEY RAILWAY.

Every Thursday and Saturday,

Until Further Notice,

COOK'S CHEAP DAY EXCURSIONS TO

SHEFFIELD,

With Bookings on Saturdays for **2** or **3** days.

From	dep. a.m.	dep. a.m.	To SHEFFIELD. Day Trip Fare.	3 2 or 3 Days on Saturdays only.
HULL—				
Cannon Street	7 0	9 40		
Beverley Road	7 4	9 44	**2/9**	**4/9**
HOWDEN	7 50	10 24		
Sheffield ... ... arr.	9 22	11 45		

The Return Train will leave Sheffield at 6-58 p.m. or 8-28 p.m. each day.

Passengers taking tickets at the higher fares must return by ordinary train leaving Sheffield at 6-58 p.m. or 8-28 p.m. on Week-days, and on Sundays at 3-34 p.m.

Every Thursday, Saturday and Sunday,

Until further notice, Cook's Cheap Return Tickets to

LITTLE WEIGHTON, SOUTH CAVE & NORTH CAVE,

Available to return from either Station on day of issue ; and to

DRAX and KIRK SMEATON,

Will be issued as under :—

FROM	Times of Starting.				Return Fares, Third Class.		
	Week-Days.			Sundays. By any ordinary stopping train in each direction.	LITTLE WEIGHTON, SOUTH CAVE and NORTH CAVE.	DRAX.	KIRK SMEATON.
HULL—	p.m.	p.m.	p.m.		Third Class.	Third Class.	Third Class.
Cannon Street ...	12 30	1 25	3 0				
Beverley Road ...	12 34	1 29	3 4		**1/-**	**1/3**	**1/9**

NOTE.—Bookings to Drax and Kirk Smeaton by 12-30 p.m. train. Bookings to Little Weighton, South and North Cave, by any of the three trains named.

BICYCLES.—Bicycle Tickets, at owner's risk are issued to Excursionists from Hull to **KIRK SMEATON** at **1/-** each return when properly labelled.

Children under 3 years of age, free ; above 3 and under 12, half-fares. The tickets are not transferable, and are available by the trains herein-named only. No luggage allowed to passengers taking day or half-day trip tickets. Passengers holding long-date tickets are allowed 60 lbs. of luggage free, under their own care, for which the Company will not be responsible.

NOTE.—The Tickets are only available to and from the Stations named above, and passengers alighting at any other Station will forfeit their tickets and be required to pay the full ordinary fare.

Should the Company consider it necessary or desirable, from any cause, to alter or cancel these arrangements, they reserve to themselves the right to do so.

A poster advertising cheap excursions to Sheffield.

In 1916 the Hull & Barnsley and Great Central Joint line opened between Aire Junction, near Hensall, and Braithwell Junction on the Midland & Great Central Joint line. Station platforms were erected at Snaith and Pollington, Sykehouse and Thorpe-in-Balne but no passenger trains ever ran. In 1922 the H&B was absorbed into the NER. This led to a number of name changes. Carlton became Carlton Towers, 'North' was added to Eastrington, and 'South' added to Howden. At the same time the nearby NER stations became South Eastrington and North Howden. At the Grouping the NER, and thus the H&B, became part of the LNER. In 1929 the passenger service between Kirk Smeaton and Wath was withdrawn, followed three years later by South Howden to Cudworth. The 1947 timetable shows four trains daily between Hull and South Howden and two only as far as North Cave, plus an early morning return to Willerby and Kirkella. There were additional services on Saturdays. These services were withdrawn on 1 August 1955, leaving the H&B as a freight-only line. In 1959 came closure to all traffic between Little Weighton and Wrangbrook Junction. The rest of the system closed progressively between 1959 and 1968. Today, just a short section of line in Hull and the branch serving Drax Power Station remains.

Mr W. Kirtley, the superintendent of the London, Chatham & Dover Railway, acted as a consultant to the H&B. He ordered forty-two locomotives of his own designs from Beyer Peacock. Matthew Stirling was appointed as Locomotive Superintendent in 1885 and was to remain in office for the remainder of the existence of the company. The remaining locomotives ordered for the railway, with one or two exceptions, were to his designs. Altogether the railway acquired 186 locomotives during its existence, all built by outside contractors. They were of the following types: 0-6-0, 2-4-0, 0-8-0 and 4-4-0 tender engines, and 0-4-0, 0-6-0 and 0-6-2 tanks. They were of fifteen different classes, built by six different manufacturers. None survived into preservation.

A timetable showing services after the withdrawal of passenger trains west of South Howden.

H&B Class B 0-6-0 No. 2518 (LNER Class J23) is seen at Barmby Moor in 1936. Originally fifty-five in number, the whole class was withdrawn by 1938. (Photo courtesy of The Transport Library)

H&B Class F2 0-6-2 No. 2486 (LNER Class N12), seen at Springhead in 1933. This engine, dating from 1901, was the last of its class to be withdrawn in 1948.

Also seen at Springhead is another design dating from 1901: H&B Class G3 0-6-0 No. 2527 (LNER Class J75). This machine lasted in service until 1949.

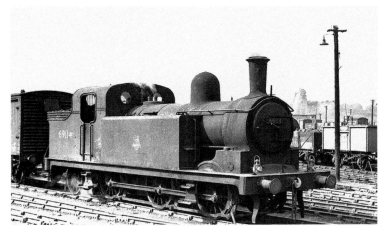

H&B Class F3 (LNER Class N13) 0-6-2 No. 69114, seen at Neville Hill in 1956. This was the last surviving H&B locomotive. It was withdrawn the same year. (Photo Peter Groom)

Barmby station in 1961, two years after closure of the line to all traffic. (Photo Ben Brooksbank)

WD 2-8-0 No. 90704 is seen at Carlton Towers on the daily pick-up freight on 28 March 1959. (Photo N. Stead, courtesy of The Transport Library)

The day of the very last pick-up freight, 3 April 1959. WD 2-8-0 No. 90571 shunts wagons at Drax Abbey. The splendid station is still in excellent condition. (Photo N. Stead, courtesy of The Transport Library)

Later the same day No. 90571 stands at the water column at Carlton Towers, ready to return to Hull. (Photo N. Stead, courtesy of The Transport Library)

Carlton Towers in 2018. The closed station sits on the short section of the H&B line retained to service the giant power station at Drax.

Along the same stretch of line is this level crossing with its H&B crossing keeper's cottage.

The Cawood, Wistow & Selby Light Railway

First mention of Cawood in connection with any railway came in 1845 when the London & York Railway (later to become the Great Northern) received the Act authorising its line north to York. It had been intended that this line would pass through Cawood and Selby. However, wiser counsel prevailed and instead the London & York agreed to use the Y&NMR route to reach York. It would be another twenty-six years before a line passed north through Selby but sadly not via Cawood. An Act of 21 July 1879 authorised the construction of the Church Fenton, Cawood & Wistow Railway, later known as the Selby & Mid-Yorkshire Union Railway. Its total length was 5.5 miles. A further Act of 1882 authorised an 8-mile extension from Wistow via Selby to meet up with the Hull & Barnsley Railway at Drax. This Act also authorised the H&BR (then still known as the Hull, Barnsley & West Riding Junction Railway & Dock Company) to work the whole line for 50 per cent of the receipts. A yet further Act of 1883 authorised a connection with the NER at Church Fenton. Unfortunately, it proved impossible to raise the capital required and all of this came to nothing.

The scheme was revived towards the end of the century and a bill was promoted by a Captain Liversedge and Mr Sebastian Meyer. The plan this time was for a line 4 miles 5 furlongs in length, connecting to the NER at a point west of Selby, continuing to Cawood, with an intermediate station at Wistow, with the railway to be known as the Cawood, Wistow & Selby Light Railway Company. The first sod was cut by Mrs Liversedge on 11 July 1896. There was very little in the way of difficulty in building the line and the railway opened on 16 February 1898. The total cost was £25,000. The first train was hauled by the company's 0-6-0 *Cawood*, hauling the company's two carriages as well as a number of NER vehicles. The train actually departed from Brayton Gates Junction, which was the railway's terminus alongside the NER Leeds–Selby line in west Selby. The train first ran to Cawood and then returned to Wistow, where luncheon was served and speeches made. The railway remained as an independent concern for only a short time, as it was purchased for £32,000 by the NER in 1900, which thereafter worked the line itself. Despite this it wasn't until 1904 that the Cawood trains were permitted to run into Selby station itself.

The station at Brayton Gates had a platform and shelter. At the junction there was also the locomotive shed, a substantial brick-built structure. From the terminus the single line ran parallel to the Leeds & Selby line for several hundred yards before turning northwards to cross the Selby–Leeds road. Some way before this crossing there was a siding connected to the branch by a forward-facing point. The Ordnance Survey map of 1905 (see page 48) appears to show some kind of structure alongside this siding, possibly a loading platform. These sidings near each location where the railway crossed a road are a feature of this line. Other sidings were south of the crossings at Crosshills Lane and Flaxley Road, and north of the crossings at Selby Common and South Lane. These sidings were presumably provided for wagons to be left and picked up later when loaded.

At Wistow, approximately 3 miles from Selby, apart from the line adjacent to the single platform, there was a more or less parallel line serving the loading bay and goods shed. There was also one other siding. The station was a substantial structure of brick, as was the goods shed. There was also a weighbridge and accompanying hut. Cawood was reached approximately 2 miles further on. The track layout here was similar to that at Wistow except that there was an additional siding. The station building was not on the platform but was at right angles to the line, facing on to Sherburn Road. The only other structures were

The inaugural train of the CW&S. The locomotive is No. 1360 *Cawood*.

In the early days of the railway *Cawood* and its train are seen at the eponymous terminus.

Another view of the locomotive, an 'L' Class 0-6-0ST built by Manning Wardle in 1897.

SELBY, WISTOW, and CAWOOD (Auto-cars—One class only).—North Eastern.															
Mls	**DOWN.**	mrn	mrn	aft	Mons	aft	aft			Mls	**UP.**	mrn	Mons	mrn	aft	aft	aft
—	Selby ....dep.	8 21	1140	3 25		5 0	7 22	...|...|...| —	Cawood ......dep.	8 52	mrn	1053	1210	3 52	7 44
3¾	Wistow	8 33	1152	3 37		5 12	7 34	...	...	1½	Wistow ......[726	8 57		1058	1215	3 57	7 49
5½	Cawood ......arr.	8 38	1157	3 42		5 17	7 39	...	...	5½	Selby 348,724,ar	9 9		1110	1227	4 9	8 1

The timetable of April 1910.

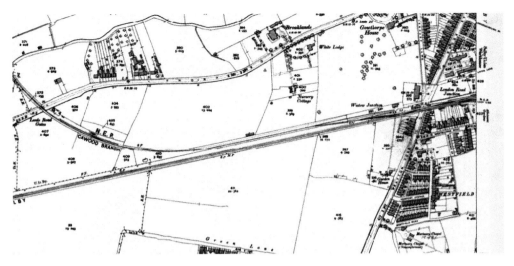

In this early map of the junction of the CW&S with the Leeds & Selby line, a building can be discerned alongside the branch and also the CW&S loco shed near Wistow Junction, as it was then named.

This is the CW&S loco shed in 1963, shortly before demolition. (Photo Roger Griffiths)

four crossing cottages at Leeds Road, Flaxley Road, Selby Common and Broad Lane. The only engineering structure of any significance was the plate-girder bridge across Selby Dam, just to the north of the Leeds Road. There was no signalling, except where the railway met the NER Leeds–Selby line, the line being worked on the one engine in steam principle.

The initial timetable was of five returns daily. Although the timetable said 'Selby', it was not the NER Selby station but the CW&S Brayton Gates station. This timetable did not last long and was superseded by a new one on 1 July 1899. Daily trips were reduced to four, with additional services on

Selby market day. Since there were two evening services to Cawood on market day, it must be assumed that one of these returned to Selby empty. Apart from the regular trains, there were occasional excursion trains. Regular passenger services ceased on 31 December 1929, although there were occasional special trains after that.

Goods traffic was heavy and consisted almost entirely of agricultural items – crops outwards, mainly potatoes, peas, grain and sugar beet, and fertilisers and manure inwards. In the early years, tank wagons of paraffin were stabled in the siding south of the Leeds Road for onward distribution by road. After the Second World War traffic went into decline and from 1945 there was just a daily trip. By the mid-1950s this train ran only as required. The end came on 2 May 1960. Shortly before this an enthusiasts' special was run using shunter D2063. Mr John Woodall of Wistow, as a boy, had travelled on the very first train and wrote to BR asking if he might travel on the very last. His wish was granted, and thus he became the last passenger ever to travel on the CW&S.

The railway had just one locomotive – a Manning Wardle 0-6-0ST of class 'L', works number 1360, constructed in 1897. It had inside cylinders with Stephenson valve gear. Driving wheels were 3 feet 6 inches in diameter. It was equipped with Westinghouse brake gear and named *Cawood*. The locomotive plus two carriages were the subject of a hire agreement with the Yorkshire Wagon Company Ltd. Shortly after the NER bought the railway on 1 January 1900 the locomotive and carriages were sold on elsewhere. *Cawood* went to work for various organisations, last being heard of in 1927, still at work. Goods wagons were hired from the NER. *Cawood* was replaced by NER H2 Class 0-6-0T No. 407 (LNER Class J79). This was a very small class of engines, just two being built by Worsdell in 1896 and a third in 1907. No. 407 had inside cylinders and driving wheels of 3 feet 5.5 inches and was fitted with larger side tanks in order to work the branch.

An interesting development took place in 1908 when two petrol-electric autocars, Nos 3170 and 3171, arrived at Selby, the duties of which included operating the Cawood branch. Both machines were altered to provide additional luggage space, reducing seating capacity from fifty-two to forty-eight. Originally fitted with Napier engines, these proved unsatisfactory and were replaced with a four-cylinder horizontally opposed Wolseley engine. The autocars were accommodated in a lean-to built alongside the coaling stage at Shelby shed. One of these cars, No. 3170, has survived into preservation after spending many years as a holiday home. It has recently been restored to working order and can be found on the Embsay & Bolton Abbey Steam Railway.

The autocars were replaced for a time by an NER 'E' Class 0-6-0T (LNER Class J71), another Worsdell design. In July 1923 a converted Leyland bus, No. 110, started work on the branch. It had a four-cylinder 35 hp petrol engine and could seat twenty-six passengers. It was later renumbered 130Y. In November 1926 the bus caught fire when it was being refuelled in the aforementioned lean-to shed and was beyond repair. For the last year of passenger services Sentinel steam railcars were used. These machines had a two-cylinder vertical engine rated at 100 hp, steam being provided by a vertical boiler. They could seat fifty-nine. They were No. 220 *Waterwitch*, No. 225 *True Blue* and No. 273 *Trafalgar*. Freight continued after closure to passengers, being hauled in later years by Classes J71, J72 and J77. At the very end a diesel shunter was used.

In 1961 the track was lifted and the bridge across Selby Dam was removed. Most of the trackbed was sold off and has disappeared under the plough or otherwise been built on. Three of the crossing keeper's cottages remain, though much altered. The disused engine shed at Brayton Gates was used for many years for locomen's Mutual Improvement Classes before being demolished in 1963. The best surviving buildings are the station building, goods shed and weighbridge hut, together with the weighbridge, at Wistow.

No. 3170 one of the petrol-electric autocars used for a time on the Cawood branch. This photograph was taken near Scarborough.

Another kind of motive power used on the branch was this Leyland bus No. 110.

After *Cawood* left the branch it was replaced by this NER 0-6-0T No. 407.

Wistow station, seen after closure. (Photo N. Stead, courtesy of The Transport Library)

The Selby to Goole Line

A notable absence from the NER tiled wall map of 1903, seen at many NER stations, is the Selby–Goole line. Perhaps by this time the NER was confident that its network was complete. In fact it was only when a rival scheme was proposed that the company finally got round to applying for its Act. Interestingly, the route of the line was almost exactly the same as the one proposed by George Hudson some sixty-five years previously. It left the Leeds – Selby line at Thorpe Gates and crossed the ECML via a bridge to reach Brayton East Junction, where there was a connecting spur to the main line. The first station was at Barlow. Here there was a connection to the Armstrong-Whitworth site, where four airships were constructed between 1917 and 1919. This site later became a Royal Artillery Ordnance Depot. The depot had its own 60 cm gauge railway system. A connection at the west end of the station gave access to a railway tip.

At Camblesforth there was just a siding accessed by a ground frame. The next station was Drax Hales, giving the little village of Drax its second station. The Hull & Barnsley station had opened in 1885. After the goods siding at Newlands came the major engineering feature of the route: the 200-foot-long girder-bridge across the River Aire. The third station on the line was Airmyn and Rawcliffe, after which the L&Y route was joined at Oakhill Junction.

The line, just 10 miles long, was double-track throughout. Built across flat, low-lying terrain, there were few difficulties in construction. Apart from the Aire river bridge there were just fourteen other bridges and one level crossing, at Barlow. The station buildings were single-storey wooden constructions. Work started in 1907 and was completed by 1910 when the first freight trains ran. Passenger services started on 1 May 1912.

The initial passenger service consisted of three Selby–Goole returns per day, with an additional train on Selby market day. Services were operated by what the NER called autocars. These were push-pull trains consisting of a locomotive and carriages. By 1916 there was a second additional train on Selby market days.

Before too long the line was singled, probably shortly after the creation of the LNER. This left the only signal box and passing place at Barlow. After the autocars came the Sentinel steam cars, introduced by the LNER in the late 1920s. In the later years the habitual motive power was in the shape of a railmotor, a G5 0-4-4T plus carriages, operating in push-pull mode. In 1947 there were four trains from Selby to Goole and five in the reverse direction. In 1957 steam gave way to Class 104 diesel multiple units. In that year there were five returns on weekdays plus an additional service on Wednesdays. It is interesting to note that the journey time of twenty-four minutes was exactly as it had been in 1916!

The end came in 1964 with the withdrawal of all services. The line from Brayton Junction to Barlow was retained until 1984 to service the tip there. The area the tip covered is now a nature reserve. Two short sections of line still remain. The first is from Brayton Junction to the civil engineering yard at Brayton East, and the second is a short length of line connecting with the former H&B line to service the power station at Drax.

Prior to the opening of the Selby–Goole line the NER had accessed Goole via Staddlethorpe (later Gilberdyke) Junction. The line from there to Goole and then on to Thorne, on the MS&L line, was opened on 30 July 1869. There was an intermediate station at Saltmarshe, named after the eponymous family, although in fact the nearest settlement was Laxton. To cross the Ouse, which at this point is 250 yards wide, a massive swing bridge was constructed. It consists of a 250-foot-long centrally pivoted swing section and five fixed spans of 116 feet. The swing section weighs some 700 tonnes and was originally moved by hydraulic power supplied by steam engines. It is now turned by electric motors.

The view towards Selby from Barlow station, seen in 1961. (Photo Ben Brooksbank)

Drax station. Wooden buildings are seen here too. (Photo N. Stead, courtesy of The Transport Library)

On 25 August 1958 G5 0-4-4T No. 67250 stands at Selby having arrived with the 11.10 from Goole. (Photo courtesy of the Railway Correspondence and Travel Society)

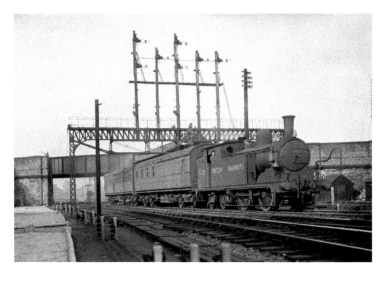

Two years earlier, the same locomotive is seen leaving Selby with a train for Goole. Notice the early BR livery. (Photo courtesy of The Transport Library)

NER Sentinel steam railcar No. 2200 *Surprise* stands outside Selby loco shed. These railcars were used on the branch in the interwar years. (Photo courtesy of the Railway Correspondence and Travel Society)

Goole station. Considerable changes have been made since this photograph was taken in 1990. Note the serpent benches, which have long since disappeared.

In 1961 Hunslet diesel No. D2599 heads through the station with a trip working to Hull. (Photo Ben Brooksbank)

WD 2-8-0 No. 90228 plods through Goole with a long rake of mineral wagons on 30 August 1960. (Photo courtesy of the Railway Correspondence and Travel Society)

In the 1950s B1 4-6-0 No. 61166 heads away from Goole with the 12.30 Hull to Doncaster service. (Photo Peter Groom)

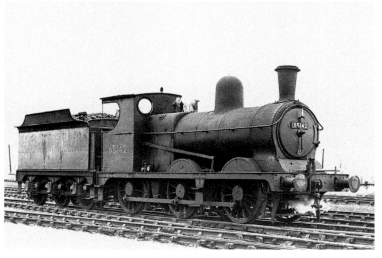

A veteran stands in the yard at Goole on 23 July 1958. MS&L 0-6-0 No. 65142 represents a design by H. Pollitt dating to the turn of the century. It was classified J10/4 by the LNER. (Photo Peter Groom)

This is the vast goods yard at Goole Docks in October 1990. All this has gone and the area is now an industrial estate.

Another view of part of the goods yard in 1990 with shunter No. 08514.

In September 2018 a Class 158 DMU rattles across Goole swing bride with a Hull–Doncaster service.

The Derwent Valley Light Railway

The Act to authorise the construction of the Derwent Valley Light Railway was obtained at the initiative of the Rural Districts of Escrick and Riccall. The Act was obtained in 1902 but it was to be another eight years before a contract was placed with Pethick Dix & Co. to construct the line at an estimated cost of £80,000. Wheldrake to Cliff Common was opened on 29 October 1912 and the remaining 4.5 miles on 19 July 1913. The railway ran from Layerthorpe, on the Foss Islands branch of the NER, to Cliff Common, where it had a joint station with the NER on the Selby–Market Weighton line. In its 16-mile length there were intermediate stations at Osbaldwick, Murton Lane, Dunnington, Elvington, Wheldrake, Cottingwith, Thorganby and Skipwith. Station buildings were all of the same style – a single-storey building in a 'cottage orné' style, with an adjacent goods shed. For the inaugural train the NER provided Class X3 2-2-4T No. 1679 together with two six-wheeled coaches. Lady Deramore performed the opening ceremony.

The timetable of 2013 showed three trains from Cliff Common to Layerthorpe, with a fourth starting from Wheldrake. There were also three trains in the other direction, with an evening train going only as far as Wheldrake. The first two trains from Layerthorpe to Cliff Common connected into Market Weighton–Selby services. Passenger numbers reached a peak in 1915 with 49,383 people carried. Numbers were holding up well in 1918 when 46,982 second-class passengers were carried, together with 564 first class. After this, a rapid decline set in, doubtless due to the competition from road transport, and in 1926, the last year of regular passenger trains, the figure for second class was just 5,381 and zero for first class.

Until 1924 the DVLR hired locomotives from the NER and its successor the LNER. In 1924 the railway purchased two Ford four-wheeled railbuses. These normally operated coupled back to back, obviating the need to be turned. For the occasions when they did operate singly, small turntables were installed at Layerthorpe and Skipwith. After the cessation of passenger services in August

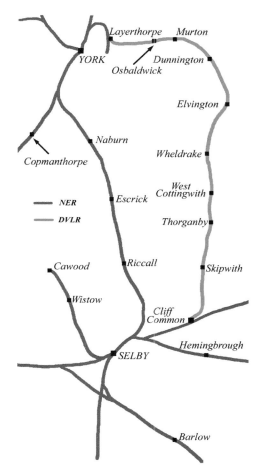

Map of the Derwent Valley Railway.

1926 the railbuses were sold to County Donegal Railways, where they were regauged to run on the 3-foot system there. In 1925, for its freight traffic, the railway purchased a Sentinel vertical-boilered locomotive of Class CE, No. 6076. The acquisition of this locomotive saw a considerable reduction in running costs but the machine was not really adequate for the task and was sold on in 1927. From then on the railway reverted to hiring in locomotives from the LNER and BR. Classes used included N12 0-6-2Ts, J71 0-6-0Ts, and J21, J24, J25 0-6-0s. In 1961 the railway started using Drewry 0-6-0 204 hp diesels (BR Class 04). In 1969 it went back once more to having its own motive power when it purchased Drewry diesels Nos 2245 and 2298 from BR. They were renumbered No. 1 and No. 2. Both these diesels survived into preservation. A third Drewry was bought for spares.

Freight traffic was essentially agricultural, and included potatoes, hay and straw, oilcake, livestock, manure, roadstone and timber. Stable manure from Leeds and Hull was transported to potato farmers and there was also a contract to transport the manure from three cavalry regiments based at Catterick Camp.

The Second World War saw the line's busiest period. A petrol depot was put in at Murton Lane; Elvington saw construction traffic for the nearby airfield; there was a mustard gas store at Cottingwith; and Wheldrake was used as a fuel depot for Operation Fido. In addition there was an increase in the normal agricultural traffic. It was said that the DVLR line was chosen for the storage of such volatile material as it could not be seen from the air, such was the extent of the surrounding leafy growth.

Just as the Derwent Valley was ignored in the Grouping, so it was when it came to nationalisation, and the railway continued as an independent concern. In the post-war years agricultural traffic continued to decline as road transport took over and the railway started to carry more in the way of bulk goods, such as grain, fuel oil, cement and coal. In 1964 BR closed the Market Weighton–Selby line, cutting off the railway's southern exit. In the light of this the decision was made to close the railway south of Wheldrake, as this section in any case generated very little traffic. The section between Wheldrake and Elvington followed in 1968, and Elvington closed in 1973. This left just the 4-mile section between Dunnington and Layerthorpe.

Passenger traffic had never been completely abandoned. A number of special trains were run, including the famous blackberry specials, and the post-war years saw a number of enthusiasts' specials. In 1977 the owners of the line decided to start running steam trains between Layerthorpe and Dunnington using J72 0-6-0T No. 69023 *Joem*. However, passenger numbers did not hold up and this activity ceased in 1979. Occasional freight trains ran along the remaining section of line but all traffic ceased in 1981, with the last train running on 27 September of that year. In 1992 a group of enthusiasts reopened a section of line at Murton Park as part of the Yorkshire Museum of Farming. The station buildings at Wheldrake were acquired and re-erected as 'Murton Park'. Trains run on Sundays and bank holidays.

The inaugural train on 19 July 1913, seen here at Elvington.

The inaugural train at Layerthorpe, having returned from Cliff Common.

Inaugural train engine NER Class X3 2-2-4T No. 1679 takes on water.

DERWENT VALLEY LIGHT RAILWAY PROVISIONAL TIMETABLE : JULY—30th SEPTEMBER, 1913.

Subject to alteration, of which due notice will be given.

WEEKDAYS—UP

		a.m.	p.m.	p.m.	p.m.	p.m.
York (Layerthorpe)	dep.	9.50	2.8	4.45	6.33	7.5
Osbaldwick		9.55	2.13	4.50	6.38	7.10
Murton Lane		9.58	2.16	4.53	6.41	7.13
Dunnington Halt		10.2	2.20	4.57	6.45	7.17
Dunnington (for Kexby)		10.6	2.24	5.1	6.49	7.21
Elvington (for Sutton)		10.12	2.30	5.7	6.55	7.27
Wheldrake		10.18	2.36	5.13	7.1	7.33
Cottingwith		10.22	2.40	5.17	S.E.	S.O.
Thorganby		10.26	2.44	5.21		
Skipwith & N. Duffield		10.31	2.49	5.26		
Cliff Common (D.V.L.)	arr.	10.38	2.56	5.33		
Cliff Common (N.E.)	dep.	10.49	3.8			
Selby (N.E.)	arr.	10.57	3.14			

WEEKDAYS—DOWN

		a.m.	a.m.	a.m.	p.m.	p.m.	p.m.
Selby (N.E.)	dep.				3.40	4.38	
Cliff Common (N.E.)	arr.				3.47	4.45	
Cliff Common (N.E.—from Market Weighton line)	arr.			10.49			
						S.E.	S.O.
Cliff Common (D.V.L.)	dep.	8.0		11.0	3.50	5.40	6.10
Skipwith & N. Duffield		8.7		11.7	3.57	5.47	6.17
Thorganby		8.12		11.12	4.2	5.52	6.22
Cottingwith		8.16		11.17	4.6	5.56	6.26
Wheldrake		8.20	8.25	11.21	4.10	6.0	6.30
Elvington (for Sutton)		TH & SO	8.31	11.27	4.16	6.6	6.36
Dunnington (for Kexby)			8.37	11.33	4.22	6.12	6.42
Dunnington Halt			8.41	11.37	4.26	6.16	6.46
Murton Lane			8.46	11.42	4.31	6.21	6.51
Osbaldwick			8.49	11.46	4.34	6.24	6.54
York (Layerthorpe)	arr.		8.53	11.50	4.38	6.28	6.58

Above: The initial timetable.

Left: Thorganby station. All the stations had the same 'wooden tea room'-type construction.

The pair of Ford railbuses that operated coupled back to back to avoid the need to turn.

The Sentinel steam engine that the railway owned for a brief period in the 1920s.

On 28 April 1938 an unidentified ex-H&B Class N12 0-6-2 is seen at Wheldrake station with a train of potatoes destined for Spain via Goole Docks.

The Railway Correspondence and Travel Society special train headed by diesel shunter No. D2111 is seen at Layerthorpe on 9 January 1965. (Photo courtesy of RCTS)

The former Wheldrake station masquerading as Murton Park on the preserved DVLR, 19 October 2018.

Freight

A glance at the 1950s map below will serve as an indication of the importance of the transport of goods by rail. Every company of any size had a rail connection. In Selby one of the largest of these companies was the British Olympia Cake Mills, which had its own internal rail system. The company originally had two 0-4-0T shunters but later the yard was shunted by BR using Selby's Y1 Sentinel tanks. After the connection to BR had been taken out the company continued to use its own internal system, utilising various machines, including a Fowler 0-4-0 diesel mechanical, a Unimog road-rail vehicle and a Trackmobile. BOCM no longer uses rail.

There were many other companies in Selby that had a rail connection. These included the Agricultural Implement Works, the Ouse Chemical Works, the

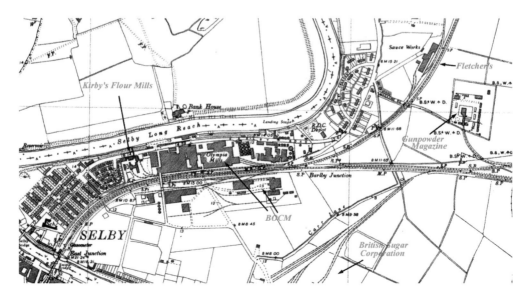

Map showing industrial railway installations north of the Ouse.

Y1 0-4-0T No. 68150 shunting at BOCM on 22 August 1958. (Photo N. Stead, courtesy of The Transport Library)

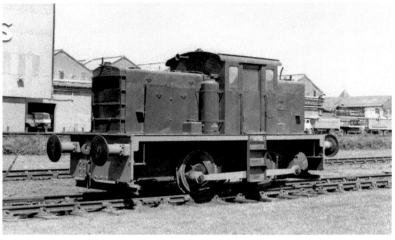

Fowler 0-4-0 shunter No. 4200003 at BOCM. This machine is now at the Embsay & Bolton Abbey Railway awaiting restoration. (Photo courtesy of Industrial Railway Society)

The Trackmobile shunting wagons under the overhead conveyor. (Photo courtesy of the Industrial Railway Society)

These rails were once part of the extensive BOCM system. Barlby signal box is in the background.

maltings, the van and wagon works, the timber yard, Fletcher's Pickle factory, Kirby's flour mills, the British Sugar Corporation, and the North Eastern Gas Board. One of the more interesting users of freight was the War Department, which had a trailing connection from the Selby–Market Weighton line to the WD gunpowder magazine, the buildings of which still exist. As well as the above there were, of course, the railway's own extensive facilities, housed in the old station building.

What is the situation today in 2018? The premises of the former British Sugar Corporation are now in the hands of the Potter Group and the rail connection survives. This is used by trains transporting limestone from the Peak District, which is used to make tarmac. Other than this, there is the Plasmor factory at Heck, which still uses rail transport. Other services that pass through Selby include trains of biomass or coal from Hull to Drax and trains of aggregates from Rylstone to Hull. Services to Heck Plasmor use the curve from Selby West to Selby Canal Junction.

The busiest stretch of railway in the area is the line from Knottingley to Drax Branch Junction, which sees all the services to and from Drax Power Station. As well as biomass and coal there are also trains of gypsum and ash, giving up to forty freight train movements per day along this line.

The Fletcher's Sauce factory. The use of rail for the transport of goods is prominently shown. The East Coast Main Line is in the foreground.

At least until the 1950s, this WD gunpowder magazine was still rail connected.

In 1957 B16 No. 61436 takes the up fast through Selby with a mixed freight. (Photo Ben Brooksbank)

On 22 August 1959 classmate No. 61465 hurries through Selby in the opposite direction with a fitted freight. (Photo N. Stead, courtesy of The Transport Library)

On 10 September 1981 English Electric Class 40 No. 40075 approaches Selby with a down parcels train.

GB Railfreight Class 66 No. 66711, resplendent in its new livery, reverses train 6E51, the 12.17 Peak Forest to Selby, into Potter's Railfreight Depot on 4 October 2018.

At Heck, EWS locomotive
No. 66177 sets back its train of
empty wagons into the Plasmor
terminal on 29 September 2018.

Train 6D72, a Hull Dairycoates to
Hexthorpe Yard empties working,
passes through Selby behind
No. 66760 on 10 July 2018.

On the same day at Hensall
No. 66755 passes with a train of
empty biomass wagons from Drax
Power Station.

Coal

The Selby Coalfield

Exploratory drilling showed that the coalfield had a potential reserve of 2 billion tonnes. Production started in 1983 with mines at Riccall, Wistow, North Selby, Stillingfleet and Whitemoor. The pit heads were carefully designed to have minimal environmental impact. Underground railways took the extracted coal to Gascoigne Wood, where it was brought to the surface and transported to the Aire Valley power stations. Peak output came in 1993/4 when 12 million tonnes were mined. By 1999 the coalfield was considered to be making a loss by the owners, UK Coal, and the mine complex ceased production in 2004. A total of 121 million tonnes had been mined.

The Aire Valley Power Stations

In the 1990s the three power stations of Ferrybridge, Eggborough and Drax produced 20 per cent of Britain's electricity. There have been three power stations at Ferrybridge. The most recent, Ferrybridge C, had a 2,000 megawatt capacity. It started production in 1966 and closed in 2016. It consumed 4 million tonnes of coal per year, supplied by an average of seventeen trains a day. The Ferrybridge Multifuel plant became operational in 2015. It burns various kinds of biomass. A further plant is planned.

Eggborough Power Station was similar in size to Ferrybridge C. It started production in 1967 and closed in March 2018. Eggborough Power Ltd has applied for permission to build a 2,000 MW gas-fired power station.

Britain's largest power station is Drax. It opened in 1973 with three generating units; by 1986 a further three units had been added, giving a total capacity of 3,870 MW. In 2011 it consumed 9.1 million tonnes of coal, supplied by an average thirty-five trains a day, six days a week. One of the principal suppliers of coal to Drax was Kellingley Colliery, the last deep mine in Britain, which closed in 2015. Other rail traffic consisted of limestone from Tunstead

No. 56086 approaches Sudforth Lane level crossing with an empty MGR train on 5 September 1992.

On the same day No. 56095 departs from Drax having delivered its trainload of coal.

On 27 February 1993 No. 56102 passes Ferrybridge signal box with a loaded MGR. Ferrybridge Power Station is seen in the background.

No. 56077 departs Milford with a loaded MGR on 3 January 1997.

In post-BR days EWS Class 66 No. 66186 passes eastbound with a train of MGR wagons.

The highly productive Kellingley Colliery was the last deep mine to close in Britain. Here we see No. 66033 pulling away from the colliery on 18 July 2002. The colliery closed in 2015.

Biomass being unloaded at Drax in September 2018. The locomotive is No. 66761 *Wensleydale Railway Association 25 Years 1990-2015.*

in Derbyshire for the gas desulphurisation plant, and the outward transport of gypsum, a by-product of gas desulphurisation. More than a million tonnes of ash was produced, much of which was sold and transported by rail. Since 2013 the power station has been in the process of being converted to burn biomass. Currently four of the six generators burn biomass. Coal is only burnt when demand is above the capacity of these four generators. To supply the biomass a new fleet of 200 wagons was constructed, each having a capacity of 71.6 tonnes. Fourteen trains a day deliver 20,000 tonnes of biomass. These trains originate at the ports of Liverpool, Tyne, Immingham or Hull.

Domestic Coal

Long before the advent of the giant power stations, coal was an essential commodity for almost every business and household. Coal was supplied to almost every station, where very often there were coal drops such as these at England Lane, near Knottingley. These were a rare survivor (overleaf), photographed in 1992, and have subsequently been demolished.

The coal drops at England Lane.

The wagons would have been shunted over the drops and the coal dropped through to the bins underneath.

Signalling

In 1969 there were signal boxes at Thorpe Gates, Selby West, Selby North, Selby South, Barlby, Barlby North, Canal, Selby Swingbridge and Brayton Junction. In 1972 Barlby was reduced to a gate box, after which the goods loops were worked by Selby South. After Selby South closed, the loops were worked by Selby West. In 1973 Selby South, Canal and Barlby North were abolished and Brayton and Thorpe Gates were reduced to gate boxes. Brayton was abolished in 1988 and Thorpe Gates in 2013. Both have been demolished. East of Selby on the line to Hull, Howden and Hemingbrough signal boxes were abolished in 1997. Gilberdyke was due to be abolished in 2016 but hung on until 23 November 2018. Saltmarshe box closed at the same time. The area is now controlled from York Integrated Electronic Control Centre.

Today just Selby, Barlby and Selby Swingbridge survive. Neither of the latter two are block posts, although the swingbridge does have signals but these are for river traffic. The swingbridge can only be operated when it is released by Selby. The latter controls all the signalling in the area, as far as Howden on the Hull line, to a point beyond Henwick Hall on the Doncaster line, and to near Hambleton Junction on the Leeds line. Selby is due to be abolished in 2019, when the whole area will come under York IECC.

The present Selby box was originally named London Road. In 1904 it became Wistow and then in 1945 Selby West. In 1973 it was reduced to a gate box and then in the same year reinstated to control all the signalling in the area, when it was renamed Selby. Today it displays the nameboard 'Selby West' but this is not correct. There have been other name changes. Selby South was originally called Selby West, and Selby North was originally Selby and later Selby East.

In 1979 a London-bound HST passes the closed Selby North signal box as it enters Selby station. (Photo courtesy of RCTS)

A view south from the road bridge at Selby with Selby South box on the left. Note the once extensive layout here. A Class 31 diesel locomotive approaches in the distance. (Photo courtesy of RCTS)

Barlby signal box dates from 1898. It is a typical NER type S1 box. It is still operational (2018) as a gate box.

Selby box (misleadingly still carrying the nameboard 'Selby West') is a very early type S1 box, though much extended. Currently controlling the whole Selby area, it is due for abolition in 2019.

Barlby North box was situated in the V between the ECML and the Market Weighton line. Here, V2 2-6-2 No. 60893 passes the box with a train from the north.

Thorpe Gates, yet another NER type S1 box. It dates from 1873 and was extended in 1907. The box has now been demolished.

This is Howden signal box, seen in 1989. As well as the section, it also controlled the level crossing and incorporates an especially large window to aid the sighting of road traffic. Howden, though now out of use, still stands as it is a listed structure.

Hensall signal box is on the Knottingley–Goole line. Although non-operational, it has been preserved as it is one of only three surviving Yardley Smith type 1 boxes. It dates from 1875.

Saltmarshe signal box is on the Gilberdyke Junction–Goole line. It is an NER type S2 dating from 1905. Note the cutaway corner to enable better sighting of road traffic. The box was abolished in November 2018.

Gascoigne Wood Junction in the 1970s. The signal box dates from 1908 and is classified as an NER type S4. It is still operational (2018). Note the lower quadrant slotted post NER signal on the right. (Photo courtesy of RCTS)

Selby Locoshed

In the early days at Selby, locomotives were stabled in part of the old station, which, as we have seen, became largely a goods depot when the new station opened in 1840. With the opening of the York–Doncaster main line in 1871 a new shed was constructed to the south-west of the station. This was of the round house type, although in a square building. It had nineteen stabling bays and a 40-foot turntable. It was completed in 1873. A second, similar building was opened in 1898. This had twenty-four bays and a 50-foot turntable. The main work for Selby's engines was hauling coal from the collieries around Pontefract and Castleford, as well as supplying the motive power for passenger and freight work on the lines to Market Weighton, Goole and Cawood. It also supplied shunting engines for the marshalling yard at Gascoigne Wood.

During BR days it had an allocation of between fifty and sixty locomotives. Its shed code was 50C, which made it a sub-shed of York. In 1950 its allocation of locomotives was still substantially NER and consisted of D20 x 13, Q5 x 4, Q6 x 15, J21 x 3, J27 x7, G5 x 2, Y1 and Y3 x 4, J71 x 1, J73 x 3, J77 x 2, A8 x 2, Q1 x 2. Loss of work and dieselisation led to the shed being closed on 13 September 1959. Just before closure on 23 August the following were present on shed: LMS 2-6-0 4MT x 6, BR 3MT 2-6-0 x 2, B16 x 5, K3 x 1, LMS 3F 0-6-0 x 1, J39 x 6, Q6 x 2, J27 x 5, J71 x 1, LMS 3F 0-6-0T x 1, D49 x 3, J50 x 3, J27 x 1, Q1 x 3, A8 x 1.

For a time after closure the shed was used as a sugar beet store. The coaling plant was demolished in November 1964 and the remaining buildings in 1965. The area was subsequently redeveloped and is now the site of a police station, municipal offices and a supermarket.

Selby loco shed, seen in 1949. (Photo John Mann collection, courtesy of the Industrial Railway Society)

A 1938 view of the shed taken from the opposite direction. The engine in the foreground is a B16 4-6-0. (Photo W. A. Camwell)

A trio of J39 0-6-0s in the shed. This was Gresley's standard goods workhorse. A total of 289 were built. (Photo N. Stead, courtesy of The Transport Library)

A view of the shed following closure. The coaling stage can be seen on the left. (Photo Roger Griffiths)

A photograph of shed staff taken in the 1880s. The locomotive is an 0-6-0 of Fletcher's 398 Class.

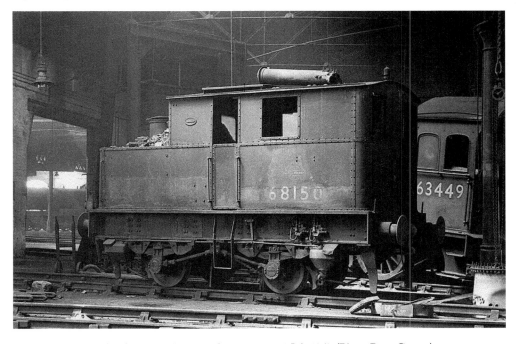

Sentinel Y1 No. 68150 taking a rest between duties, seen on 8 July 1958. (Photo Peter Groom)

J77 0-6-0 No. 68406 was a rebuild of Fletcher's G6 0-4-4WT design, dating from 1874. (Photo Peter Groom)

No. 2136 *Hope*, one of the Sentinel steam railcars, stands outside the shed. (Photo courtesy of The Transport Library)

Vincent Raven introduced the B16 4-6-0 design in 1918. A total of seventy were built. This is No. 797 in LNER days. (Photo courtesy of The Transport Library)

In the foreground is G5 0-4-4 No. 67286, one of Selby's stalwarts on the Goole branch. Behind is an Ivatt 4MT 2-6-0. These engines were popularly known a 'Flying Pigs'. (Photo Peter Groom)

Wilson Worsdell only built ten of this 0-6-0 shunter, LNER Class J77. This is No. 68357, seen at the shed on 11 July 1956. (Photo Peter Groom)

Selby's T1 4-8-0T No. 69915 was used to shunt the yard at Gascoigne Wood Marshalling Yard. (Photo Peter Groom)

Q1 No. 69931 was another powerful tank used at Gascoigne Wood. These machines were in fact rebuilds of Robinson's Q4 0-8-0 built for the GCR. (Photo Peter Groom)

The coal stage, seen in 1963. (Photo Roger Griffiths)

Selby Station Past and Present

SELBY STATION

45

A view of Selby station probably taken round the turn of the century. Note the two centre lines for through trains.

Taken in early LNER days, B13 4-6-0 No. 748 arrives from the south with a long rake of mineral wagons. (Photo courtesy of The Transport Library)

In the summer of 1964 K1 2-6-0 No. 62061 pulls away from the yard with a short engineering train. (Photo courtesy of RCTS)

This 1970s view, taken from the road bridge, shows how the railway has changed. The goods yard is empty, the semaphore signals have been replaced by colour lights and the platforms are occupied by diesel multiple units. (Photo courtesy of RCTS)

Standing at Selby on 10 September 1981 with the 12.05 Kings Cross to York is 'Deltic' No. 55021. Notice that the two through lines are still extant.

A view of the decorative canopy ironwork on platform 2, one of the reasons for the station having listed status.

A Northern Trains Hull–York service crosses the swing bridge as it arrives at the station on 6 July 2018.

On the same day a Hull Trains 'Adelante' unit arrives with the 08.23 Hull to Kings Cross.

A visitor from the past. No. 20007 heads train 37OV, the 11.40 Sheffield to Hull rail head cleaning train, through Selby on 1 November 2018. This locomotive is more than sixty years old. The other engine is No. 20205.